THE NORTH AFRICA COOKBOOK

TASTE EASY, DELICIOUS & AUTHENTIC
AFRICAN RECIPES | MADE EASY.

JAMIE WOODS

CONTENTS

DELECTABLE DESSERT RECIPES FROM NORTH AFRICA

INTRODUCTION

What are the best ways for you to create tasty North Africa dishes with ingredients that are the same or quite similar to those used in the region of the world?

Just thumb through the amazing and exotic recipes in this illustrated cookbook.

How do African ingredients lend themselves to delicious meals in other parts of the world?

North Africa has various food sources, bordered by the desert and ocean, and close in proximity to the Middle East, with which it shares some of its spices. The first tribes of Africa were the inventors of couscous, and they lived largely on wheat, lentils, fava beans & honey, until the ships began arriving with new ingredients to trade.

The traditional foods are prominent to this day in Northern Africa. They use olives & olive oil, lemons, garlic, onions, dates, oranges and lamb, along with harissa sauce/paste. Their largest meal is typically lunch, eaten during the afternoon hours. They enjoy vegetable salads, couscous and Arabian-style cheese and flatbreads.

Tagine dishes are symbolic in Northern Africa. They are

made with vegetables, meat or fish, and they usually are spiced well and thick in consistency.

You can spice up your everyday meals by including harissa and other North African spices in your lunches and dinners. Make the wonderful dishes your own. Read on to learn more...

NORTH AFRICAN BREAKFAST RECIPES

EGG & BEAN BREAKFAST

Eggs and beans make this wonderfully hearty and filling breakfast dish. You can also serve the North African recipe for brunch or lunch.

Makes: 4 Servings

Cooking + Prep Time: 45 minutes

Ingredients:

- 1 tbsp. of oil, olive
- 2 thinly sliced capsicums, red
- 2 thinly sliced onions, brown
- 3 thinly sliced cloves of garlic
- 1 x 14-oz. can of tomatoes, diced

•1 x 14-oz. can of rinsed and drained four bean mix
•1 & 1/2 tsp. of paprika, smoked + more for sprinkling
•4 eggs, large

Instructions:

1. Heat the oil in non-stick, deep frying pan on high. Stir while cooking the capsicums till softened, about 5 minutes. Add garlic and onion. Stir while cooking till softened and browned, 10 minutes.

2. Stir in the tomatoes, paprika, beans & 1/3 cup of filtered water. Bring to boil. Lower heat level, then cover pan. Simmer for 8-10 minutes.

3. Use a large spoon to make four holes in the bean mixture. Crack one egg in each of the holes. Cover pan. Cook till whites of eggs have set, 5 minutes. Sprinkle with more paprika, if desired, and serve.

TUNISIA EGGS & TOMATOES

This is a hearty African breakfast that's still easy to prepare. The tomato sauce is pleasingly fragrant as it cooks, and the shakshuka is an amazing breakfast.

Makes: 2-3 Servings

Cooking + Prep Time: 35 minutes

Ingredients:

- •2 tbsp. of oil, olive
- •1 diced onion, mild
- •1 sliced bell pepper, red
- •1 sliced bell pepper, green
- •3 minced garlic cloves

- •4 diced tomatoes, ripe
- •1 tsp. of cumin, ground
- •1 tsp. of paprika, ground
- •1/2 tsp. of chili powder
- •3/4 tsp. of salt, kosher
- •4 eggs, large

Instructions:

1. In cast-iron, large skillet with lid, heat the oil on med-high. Add the onion. Sauté till softened, 2 or 3 minutes. Add garlic and peppers. Sauté for 3 to 5 more minutes.

2. Add tomatoes, paprika, cumin, chili powder and kosher salt. Combine well. Bring mixture to simmer. Reduce heat level to med-low. Leave skillet uncovered and continue simmering for 10 to 15 minutes, till mixture is as thick as you desire. Taste and adjust seasonings, if desired.

3. Make four indentations in mixture and crack eggs into indentations. Cover skillet. Simmer till eggs set, 5 to 7 minutes. Serve promptly.

EGYPTIAN TAHINI FAVA BEAN BREAKFAST

This dish is also known as ful medames, and it includes fava beans stewed along with tahini. The beans are seasoned using lemon, garlic and cumin.

Makes: 3-4 Servings

Cooking + Prep Time: 15 minutes

Ingredients:

- •3 garlic cloves
- •1 tsp. of toasted cumin seeds
- •Salt, kosher, as desired
- •3 tbsp. of tahini
- •2 x 15-oz. cans of beans, fava

•2-3 tbsp. of lemon juice, freshly squeezed + extra if desired

Instructions:

1. Add pinch of kosher salt to garlic and cumin seeds in mortar & pestle. Crush till seeds have cracked & garlic is in tiny chunks.

2. Add fava beans and their liquid in med. pan. Combine with garlic and tahini paste. Stir frequently while cooking on med-high for 5 minutes or so, till liquid retains a bit of broth-like traits, but is turning thicker.

3. Add the fresh squeezed lemon juice & kosher salt, as desired. Mash 1/3 of fava beans to make the mixture thicker. Serve with pita bread.

NORTH AFRICAN RECIPES FOR LUNCH, DINNER, APPETIZERS AND SIDE DISHES

LAMB MEATBALLS WITH EGG TAGINE

Paprika and cumin spiced lamb meatballs, called kefta, make this dish pop. The Kalamata olives and baked eggs give the dish an elegant touch.

Makes: 8 Servings

Cooking + Prep Time: 1 hour & 15 minutes

Ingredients:

- 1 pound of lamb, ground
- 1 & 1/2 tbsp. of cumin, ground
- 1 & 1/2 tbsp. of paprika, ground
- Salt, kosher & pepper, black, as desired
- 4 tbsp. of butter, unsalted

•2 tbsp. of oil, olive

•4 minced garlic cloves

•1 minced large onion, yellow

•1 tsp. of chili flakes, red, crushed

•1/2 tsp. of ginger, ground

•1/2 tsp. of saffron threads, crushed

•1 bay leaf, medium

•1 x 28-oz. can of peeled, whole tomatoes, juice drained, hand-crushed

•4 eggs, large

•1/2 cup of un-pitted olives, kalamata

•1/4 cup of parsley, finely chopped

Instructions:

1. Add the lamb plus 1 tbsp. each paprika and cumin to bowl. Season as desired. Mix till combined evenly. Form this mixture in 12 balls of 1 oz. each. Place them on a medium plate. Chill till you need them.

2. Heat oil and butter in large pot on med-high. Add onions and garlic. Stir while cooking for 4-5 minutes, till soft. Add remainder of paprika and cumin, plus ginger, chili flakes, bay leaf and saffron.

3. Stir while cooking for 2-3 minutes, till mixture is fragrant. Add the tomatoes. Stir while cooking for 8-10 minutes till sauce has been reduced a bit and till tomatoes have broken down. Add the meatballs. Cover and cook for 10 minutes, till cooked fully through.

4. Crack the eggs over top of mixture. Arrange the olives around them. Cover pot. Continue to cook for 8-9 minutes, till whites have cooked & yolks are still a bit runny. Remove cover from the pot. Use parsley to sprinkle. Serve.

5

CLASSIC BABA GHANOUSH

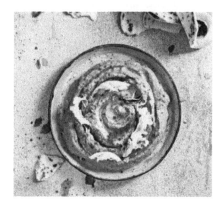

This is a delicious recipe for the traditional dip made with eggplant. Use pita bread to dip in it, and you'll have a light and delicious appetizer.

Makes: 3 Servings

Cooking + Prep Time: 55 minutes

Ingredients:

- •1 eggplant, large
- •4 smashed garlic cloves
- •1 & 1/2 tbsp. of tahini sauce

- •1/2 fresh lemon, juice only
- •Optional: 1/2 tsp. of pepper flakes, red
- •Salt, kosher, as desired
- •1 tbsp. of oil, olive, +/- as desired
- •To garnish: a pinch of parsley flakes, dried

Instructions:

1. Preheat the oven to 400F. Arrange racks with one high and one low.

2. Cut shallow slit through side of eggplant. Place in casserole dish.

3. Roast eggplant in 400F oven on low rack for 35-40 minutes, till eggplant is fully soft and shrunken. Move casserole dish to the high rack. Continue to bake about 5 more minutes, till skin has become charred. Allow eggplant to cool till you can handle it.

4. Peel eggplant skin and discard. Place eggplant in medium or large bowl. Add tahini, lemon juice, garlic, pepper flakes & kosher salt. Stir till the ingredients have mixed evenly. Drizzle baba ghanoush with oil. Use parsley to garnish and serve.

TUNISIAN GREENS WITH BRAISED VEAL

Also known as molokhia, this vegetable dish is often used frozen or fresh in Northern Africa. Tunisians, however, use a dried and ground version for the tasty dish.

Makes: 6 Servings

Cooking + Prep Time: 4 hours & 45 minutes

Ingredients:

• 3/4 oz. of molokhia leaves, dried
• 2/3 cup + 1 tbsp. of oil, olive
• 2/3 cup of powdered molokhia
• 1/4 cup of tomato paste, no salt added
• 2 tbsp. of garlic, minced finely

- 2 tsp. of harissa paste + extra to serve, as desired
- 1 tsp. of coriander, ground
- 1 tsp. of caraway, ground
- Salt, kosher, as desired
- 1/2 tsp. of pepper, ground
- 2 pounds of 2" cubed veal, boneless
- To serve: lemon wedges, fresh
- To serve: crusty bread like baguette or similar

Instructions:

1. In spice grinder, grind leaves of molokhia into powder.

2. Add 8 cups filtered water to large pan. Bring to low boil. Set heat-proof measuring cup near stove.

3. In large pot on low heat level, combine oil & molokhia. Allow to cook till lightly sizzling and bubbling. Immediately whisk in 1 cup boiling, filtered water. When incorporated fully, whisk in second cup of boiling water.

4. Raise heat level to med. Whisk in remainder of boiling water and bring mixture to simmer. Reduce heat level to med-low. Cover pot. Cook for 2 – 2 & 1/2 hours while stirring once every 15 minutes so bottom won't burn, till mixture is very dark blackish-green in color.

5. Whisk in garlic, tomato paste, coriander, harissa, caraway, 1 pinch kosher salt & 1/2 tsp. of ground pepper. Add veal. Raise heat level to med-high and bring mixture back to simmer. Reduce heat level to med-low. Leave pot uncovered and continue to cook, stirring once every 15 minutes, till meat becomes tender. Sauce should reduce by 2/3 and thicken, 1 & 3/4 – 2 hours.

6. Adjust seasoning as desired. Ladle stew into individual bowls. Serve with extra harissa, lemon wedges & crusty bread, as desired.

NORTH AFRICAN CRUSTED LAMB

This crusted lamb is a simple twist on the traditional preparation of lamb. You'll coat the lamb with honey and molasses and spices commonly used in North Africa. It goes especially well with couscous.

Makes: Various # of Servings

Cooking + Prep Time: 45 minutes

Ingredients:

- 1/2 cup of shelled pistachio nuts, unsalted
- 1/2 tbsp. of sesame seeds, toasted
- 1 tbsp. of coriander, ground
- 1/4 tsp. of cumin, ground

- •1/2 tsp. of sugar, granulated
- •1/4 tsp. of salt, kosher
- •1 tbsp. of molasses, pomegranate
- •1 tbsp. of honey, pure
- •16 well-trimmed lamb rib chops, small
- •1 tbsp. of oil, vegetable

Instructions:

1. Add first six ingredients from above list to a food processor. Turn on and off, blending intermittently, till mixture has the consistency of breadcrumbs. Transfer this mixture, known as "dukkha", to a shallow bowl and set it aside for now.

2. Whisk honey and molasses in separate small bowl and set it aside.

3. Season chops as desired. Heat the oil in large, heavy skillet on med-high. Add 1/2 of chops to skillet. Cook till done as you desired, usually two minutes each side if you prefer med-rare. Transfer chops to a plate and tent them using foil, so they'll stay warm. Repeat these steps with the rest of the lamb chops.

4. Hold bone ends of chops and dip each side of the meat in the dukkah mixture, coating well. Transfer chops to a platter. Drizzle with honey mixture and serve.

8

BEET & TAHINI DIP

The luxurious nutty taste of tahini is not only useful in hummus. It gives this bright red dip a unique taste that everyone loves.

Makes: 2-3 Servings

Cooking + Prep Time: 1 hour & 10 minutes

Ingredients:

- 1 pound of trimmed beets, fresh
- 1/2 cup of tahini
- 2 garlic cloves, medium
- 3 tbsp. of lemon juice, fresh
- 3 ice cubes

•Salt, kosher & pepper, ground, as desired
•For garnishing: 1 tbsp. of oil, olive
•For garnishing: Small handful of toasted pine nuts
•For serving: pita or similar bread to dip

Instructions:

1. Bring medium-sized pan of filtered water to boil. Add the beets. Cook for an hour or so, till they are tender.

2. Drain beets and peel them. Place in food processor with tahini, garlic, lemon juice & cubed ice. Season as desired. Puree till smooth. Spoon into medium bowl. Garnish using oil & pine nuts and serve with bread for dipping.

9

MOROCCAN VEGETABLE STEW

This easy stew is an excellent base for using up cooked meat from your refrigerator. It freezes well and tastes just as wonderful when thawed and prepared as a leftover.

Makes: 4 Servings

Cooking + Prep Time: 1 hour & 20 minutes

Ingredients:

- 2 tbsp. of oil, sunflower or olive
- 1 finely sliced onion, large
- 1 tsp. of cumin, ground
- 2 tbsp. of harissa paste
- 1 x 14-oz. can of tomatoes, chopped

•1 x 14-oz. can of drained, rinsed lentils or chickpeas

•2 & 1/2 cups of stock or filtered water

•Salt, kosher & black pepper, as desired

Instructions:

1. Heat oil in large pan. Fry onion slices gently, while regularly stirring, till lightly browned and softened, 6 to 8 minutes. Add harissa and cumin. Stir constantly while cooking for a minute longer.

2. Add tomatoes to pan. Bring to simmer. Stir constantly while cooking for two minutes.

3. Tip in lentils or chickpeas. Stir in stock or water. Bring to simmer. Stir occasionally while cooking for five minutes. Season as desired. Serve.

10

PEARL ONION & VEAL PIE

This meat pie is a staple in North Africa, often made using poultry. The recipe uses veal instead, along with pearl onions, for a unique and tasty meat pie.

Makes: 8 Servings

Cooking + Prep Time: 2 hours & 55 minutes

Ingredients:

• 10 tbsp. of melted butter, unsalted
• 3 tbsp. of oil, olive
• 1 pound of peeled onions, pearl
• 2 & 3/4 pounds of deboned, 2" cubed veal shank
• Salt, kosher & ground pepper, as desired

- 1 tsp. of allspice, ground
- 1 tsp. of nutmeg, grated
- 1 stemmed, de-seeded, finely chopped chili, serrano
- 4 cups of stock, chicken or veal
- 16 sheets of dough, phyllo

Instructions:

1. In large pan with a heavy bottom, heat 2 tbsp. oil & butter on med. heat. Add onions and stir while cooking for 10 minutes, till caramelized. Transfer onions to medium bowl.

2. Raise heat level to med-high. Season veal as desired. Add to pan. Turn while cooking for 10-12 minutes, till all sides have browned.

3. Stir in serrano chili, allspice and nutmeg. Stir while cooking for a minute, till fragrant. Return onions to pot and add stock. Bring to boil. Then reduce heat level to low. Stir occasionally while cooking for an hour and 15-20 minutes, till veal has become tender. Remove from heat. Allow to cool and shred meat roughly.

4. Heat oven to 350F. Brush inside of 9" springform with some butter.

5. Line pan bottom with a sheet of phyllo. Allow the excess to hang over sides. Brush with more melted butter. Repeat the layers with seven more sheets of phyllo, and brush with butter between each. Rotate sheets of phyllo 1/4 turn per layer so they are over-lapped in pan.

6. Scrape veal & onions in pan. Spread in even layer. Fold over-hanging phyllo sheets back in over veal. Brush with additional butter. Repeat the layering with last eight sheets of phyllo atop filling and brush with butter between them. Rotate 90 degrees per layer so they, too, overlap. Tuck phyllo edges in pan. Brush pie top with more butter.

7. Bake in 350F oven for 35-40 minutes, till golden brown. Transfer to rack and allow meat pie to cool, then serve.

NORTH AFRICAN VEGETABLE TAGINE

This Moroccan tagine is filled with the flavors of North Africa. It's simple to make but can be served at dinner parties as it has an impressive presentation.

Makes: 4 Servings

Cooking + Prep Time: 1 & 1/4 hours

Ingredients:

• 1 x 14-oz. can of rinsed, drained chickpeas
• 1/4 pint of stock, vegetable
• 3 & 1/2 oz. of roughly chopped apricots, dried
• 2 sliced onions, large
• 2 crushed garlic cloves

- •2 tbsp. of oil, olive + extra for cauliflower roasting
- •1/2 tsp. of turmeric, ground
- •1/2 tsp. of ginger, ground
- •1/2 tsp. of cumin, ground
- •1/2 tsp. of coriander, ground
- •1/2 tsp. of salt, kosher
- •1 pound & 7 oz. of florets, cauliflower
- •For serving
- •7 oz. of couscous – cook using directions on package
- •2 tbsp. of almonds, roasted & flaked
- •1 tbsp. of chopped coriander, fresh

Instructions:

1. Preheat oven to 425F.

2. Place all ingredients with exception of cauliflower in large pan. On high heat, bring to boil. Reduce heat level to med-low and cover pan. Stir occasionally while gently simmering for 30-35 minutes.

3. Place florets of cauliflower in large-sized roasting tray. Use oil to drizzle them, then sprinkle with kosher salt, as desired. Roast in 425F oven till golden and tender, 35 to 30 minutes.

4. Add roasted cauliflower florets to simmering tagine. Simmer for about five minutes. Season as desired. Sprinkle with coriander and almond flakes. Serve alongside couscous, if you like.

SPICED COUSCOUS WITH CARROTS & FENNEL

This Israeli-inspired dish is given a fresh new feel through the use of ras el hanout, which is a spice blend from North Africa. It's a simple meal that's filling and delicious.

Makes: 4 Servings

Cooking + Prep Time: 35 minutes

Ingredients:

- 2 tbsp. of oil, olive
- 2 finely chopped garlic cloves
- 1 shallot, chopped finely
- 1 x 1/2"-cut carrot, medium
- 1 trimmed, 1/2"-cut bulb of fennel – reserve fronds for garnishing

- 1 cup of couscous, Israeli-style
- 2 cups of stock, chicken
- 1/3 cup of cilantro, chopped finely
- 1/3 cup of mint, chopped finely
- 2 tbsp. of ras el hanout, bottled
- 1 halved, de-seeded, 1/2"-cut cucumber
- 2 fresh oranges, squeezed juice and grated zest
- Salt, kosher & pepper, ground, as desired

Instructions:

1. Heat the oil in large pan on med-high heat. Add shallot and garlic, and cook till soft, about 2 minutes. Add fennel and carrot, and cook for 3 more minutes.

2. Add the couscous, toasting for 2 minutes or so. Add the stock and bring to boil, then reduce the heat level and cover the pan. Simmer for 12 to 15 minutes, till couscous is tender.

3. Stir in mint, cilantro, cucumber, ras el hanout, orange juice and zest. Season as desired. Transfer to large platter. Use fennel fronds to garnish and serve.

NORTH AFRICAN MINT TEA

Hot tea with mint is a Moroccan favorite served any time of the day. Many people love the tea cold, too, made by allowing the tea to completely cool and straining it into glasses filled with ice.

Makes: 4 Servings

Cooking + Prep Time: 20 minutes

Ingredients:
- 1 quart of water, boiling + extra to heat teapot
- 3 bags of tea, green, or 1 tbsp. of green tea, loose
- 3/4 cup of sugar, granulated

•3 cups of crushed, packed mint stems and leaves + 4 sprigs to garnish

Instructions:

1. Add just a bit of boiling hot water to large teapot. Swish around so pot is heated, then pour it out.

2. Add tea to teapot. Add 1 cup boiling water. Cover pot. Allow to steep for 3-4 minutes.

3. Add mint stems & leaves and sugar to teapot. Add last 3 cups of boiling water. Cover pot. Allow to steep for 4-5 minutes. Stir well. Continue steeping for 5 more minutes. Strain into tea cups or glasses of ice. Serve.

14

MOROCCAN CUMIN & PEPPER CARROTS

Cumin, fresh mint and pepper are the main flavor-makers in this carrot salad. The dressing is lightly sweetened and provides added taste.

Makes: 4-6 Servings

Cooking + Prep Time: 35 minutes + 2 hours chilling time

Ingredients:
- 1 & 1/2 pounds of carrots, baby
- 1 tsp. of salt, kosher + extra as desired
- 1 minced garlic clove

- 1/4 cup of oil, olive
- 2 tbsp. of lemon juice, fresh
- 2 tbsp. of mint, chopped roughly
- 1 tsp. of pepper, Aleppo
- 1 tsp. of cumin, ground
- 1 tsp. of sugar, granulated

Instructions:

1. Place carrots in deep-sided 10" skillet. Add 1 & 1/2 cups of filtered water. Season carrots as desired with kosher salt. Bring to boil. Cook carrots and turn as needed, for 8-10 minutes, till they have barely started softening. Transfer carrots to work surface. Allow them to cool. Cut in halves.

2. Return skillet to heat. Add garlic. Boil till cooking liquid is syrupy and reduced to 2 to 4 tbsp., which should take 3-4 minutes. Remove skillet from heat. Whisk in 1 tsp. kosher salt, then lemon juice, oil, Aleppo, mint, sugar and cumin.

3. Pour dressing into large-sized bowl. Stir in carrots and coat evenly. Cover bowl with cling wrap. Place in refrigerator for 2 hours or longer. Serve.

15

NORTH AFRICAN COUSCOUS AND CHICKEN SOUP

This is a popular dish in its native Morocco, even though it's not a quick recipe to make. Combining its ingredients into a soup helps to save time and makes the dish even more flavorful.

Makes: 4 Servings

Cooking + Prep Time: 40 minutes

Ingredients:

- •2 tbsp. of oil, cooking
- •1 chopped onion, medium
- •1 lb. of strip-cut chicken thighs, skinless, boneless

- 1/4 tsp. of cayenne
- 1 tsp. of cumin, ground
- 1 & 3/4 tsp. of salt, kosher
- 1/4 tsp. of pepper, ground
- 1 peeled, cubed sweet potato, 1/2 lb. or so
- 1 lengthways quartered, 1"-crossways cut zucchini, fresh
- 3/4 cup of pureed tomatoes
- 1 quart of water, filtered
- 2 cups of chicken broth, canned, low-sodium
- 1/3 cup of chopped parsley, fresh
- 1/2 cup of couscous

Instructions:

1. Heat oil on medium heat in large-sized pot. Add onion. Stir occasionally while cooking for 4-5 minutes, till translucent.

2. Raise heat to med-high. Add chicken, cumin, cayenne, kosher salt & ground pepper to pot. Stir occasionally while cooking for 2-3 minutes.

3. Stir in sweet potato, tomato puree, zucchini, water & chicken broth. Bring to boil. Reduce heat, then stir occasionally while simmering for 9-10 minutes, till vegetables become tender.

4. Add couscous. Stir occasionally while simmering for 4-5 minutes. Remove pot from heat. Cover soup and let it set for 2-3 minutes. Add parsley. Serve.

16

CAULIFLOWER & LAMB STEW

This stew is rich in the flavors of North African spices. The cauliflower stems will be minced, then sautéed, and their florets will be broiled and added for the texture.

Makes: 4-6 Servings

Cooking + Prep Time: 3 & 1/4 hours

Ingredients:

• 5 tbsp. of oil, olive
• 4 tbsp. of melted butter, unsalted

•2 pounds of trimmed, 2-inch cut lamb shoulder, boneless

•Salt, kosher & pepper, black, as desired

•5 minced garlic cloves

•3 cored, minced tomatoes, plum

•2 minced large onions, red

•1/2 head of cauliflower – cut in large-sized florets; peel and mince the stems

•1/3 cup of white wine, dry

•1/4 cup of tomato paste, no salt added

•2 tsp. of cumin, ground

•1 tsp. of cinnamon, ground

•5 cups of stock, chicken or lamb

•2 tbsp. of corn starch – mix w/2 tbsp. of cold, filtered water

•1/3 cup of harissa, bottled

•8 roughly chopped dates, pitted

•1/2 tsp. of paprika, smoked

•1/4 cup of toasted almonds, sliced

Instructions:

1. Heat 2 tbsp. of butter and the oil in large pan on med-high heat. Work in batches to season the lamb as desired and cook for 18-20 minutes, turning so all sides brown. Transfer lamb cubes to plate.

2. Add the tomatoes, garlic, cauliflower stems and onions to the pan. Cook for 8 to 10 minutes, till golden. Add the wine, cumin, cinnamon and tomato paste and cook for 3-4 minutes.

3. Add lamb and stock and boil. Reduce the heat level to med-low. Cover pan. Cook for 2 hours +/- till lamb meat is quite tender.

4. Add corn starch mixture and stir. Return mixture to boil. Reduce the heat level to med. Stir in dates, harissa, kosher salt & black pepper. Cook for 5 more minutes.

5. Heat the oven broiler.

6. Stir remainder of butter along with smoked paprika in medium bowl. Season as desired. Place the florets of cauliflower on cookie sheet. Toss with the paprika-spiced butter. Stir as

needed while broiling for 8-10 minutes, till florets are chewy and a bit charred.

7. Ladle the stew in individual bowls. Use almonds and florets to garnish and serve.

NORTH AFRICAN HARISSA BUTTERNUT SQUASH

This butternut squash dish is tantalizingly flavored with harissa, a North African sauce. You can find it in jars online and in international food stores.

Makes: 6 Servings

Cooking + Prep Time: 1 hour & 50 minutes

Ingredients:

- •1 garlic clove, whole
- •2 thickly sliced garlic cloves
- •Salt, kosher, as desired
- •1 tbsp. of tomato paste, no salt added
- •1 tsp. of lemon juice, fresh squeezed

- 1 tbsp. of chili powder, ancho
- 1 tbsp. of paprika, smoked
- 1/4 tsp. of pepper, cayenne
- 1/4 tsp. of cumin, ground
- 1/4 tsp. of ground caraway seeds
- 1/2 cup of oil, olive
- 1 & 1/2 lb. of peeled, de-seeded, 1" chunk-cut squash, butternut
- 2 tbsp. of water, filtered
- Pepper, black, as desired

Instructions:

1. Preheat oven to 375F.

2. Mash whole clove of garlic with chef knife flat side, making a paste. Season as desired. Scrape into small-sized bowl & stir in lemon juice and tomato paste.

3. Add paprika, chili powder, cumin, cayenne & caraway. Stir in 1/4 cup + 2 tbsp. oil gradually. Season as desired.

4. Toss squash in medium bowl with 2 tbsp. harissa and sliced garlic. Add water and last 2 tbsp. oil. Season as desired. Spread squash in one layer in 8x8" casserole dish. Roast in middle of oven till squash becomes tender and has browned in some spots, which usually takes an hour and 15-20 minutes. Serve.

18

MOROCCAN STUFFED SARDINES

Either canned or fresh sardines will work in this crispy and spicy snack. It includes many of the favorite flavors of Morocco.

Makes: 4-6 Servings

Cooking + Prep Time: 1 hour & 10 minutes

Ingredients:

- Chermoula spice blend, bottled
- 12 cleaned sardines, heads removed, fresh or canned
- 1/2 cup of oil, olive
- 1 cup of semolina, fine
- 2 tsp. of cumin, ground
- 1 tsp. of paprika, smoked

•3 beaten eggs, large
•Salt, kosher, as desired
•To serve: lemon wedges, fresh

Instructions:

1. To stuff sardines, splay them open with your fingers. Pinch spines and pull towards tails. Snap off from just above the tails and discard spines. Spread 1/2 tbsp. of chermoula on inside of 1/2 of sardines. Top those with remainder of sardines. Secure using toothpicks. Transfer the sardines to plate and chill for 20 minutes.

2. Heat the oil in 12-inch skillet on med-high. Whisk cumin, semolina and paprika in shallow bowl. Place the eggs in separate bowl.

3. Hold sardine tails and work in small batches to dip them in eggs and semolina. Fry the sardines and flip them once, till crisp and golden. Transfer them to a plate lined with paper towels and let them drain. Serve with fresh lemon wedges.

19

NORTH AFRICAN GARLIC EGGPLANT SALAD

This silky and intense-flavor version of the popular dish ratatouille is prepared with sweetened or spiced cooked mashed vegetables. It makes a wonderful appetizer.

Makes: 6 Servings

Cooking + Prep Time: 55 minutes

Ingredients:

•2 lb. of peeled, lengthwise quartered then crosswise halved eggplants, small

•6 halved garlic cloves, medium

•2 tbsp. of oil, olive

•1 x 28-oz. can of plum tomatoes, peeled, chopped coarsely – reserve the juice

•1/2 cup of cilantro, chopped coarsely

•1 tsp. of cumin, ground

•1 tsp. of paprika, sweet

•1/8 tsp. of red pepper, crushed

•2 tbsp. of lemon juice, fresh

•Salt, kosher & pepper, ground, as desired

Instructions:

1. In large pan with steamer basket fitted, bring a half-inch of filtered water to simmer. Add eggplant, then garlic to steamer. Cover pan. Steam on med. heat for 18-20 minutes, till tender.

2. In deep, large skillet, heat oil. Add tomatoes and juice, cumin, cilantro, red pepper and paprika. Stir occasionally while cooking on med-high for 13-15 minutes, till thickened.

3. Drain steamed eggplant with garlic in colander. Press gently, extracting excess water. Transfer to bowl. Mash garlic finely and eggplant coarsely. Scrape into tomato sauce in skillet.

4. Add lemon juice to skillet. Stir occasionally while simmering on med. heat for five minutes. Season eggplant as desired. Transfer to serving bowl. Can be served at room temp. or chilled lightly.

20

TAGINE LEMON PASTA

The spicy flavors of Moroccan tagine come together in this pasta salad, with cinnamon, olive and lemon. It can be served as a side or tossed with shredded meat for an entrée.

Makes: 4-6 Servings

Cooking + Prep Time: 15 minutes

Ingredients:

- 1 finely chopped onion, small
- 2 tbsp. of lemon juice, fresh
- 2 cups of cooked, cooled couscous, Israeli-style
- 1 finely chopped carrot, medium
- 1/2 cup of pitted, chopped olives, green

- •1/2 cup of minced lemon, preserved
- •1/4 cup of oil, olive
- •1/2 tsp. of cinnamon, ground
- •1/2 tsp. of cumin, ground
- •1/2 tsp. of ginger, ground
- •Salt, kosher & pepper, cracked, as desired
- •2 tbsp. of chopped parsley, fresh

Instructions:

1. Soak onion in fresh lemon juice for 3-5 minutes, quick-pickling onions.

2. In large-sized bowl, combine all ingredients. Toss them together and season as desired. Serve.

21

NORTH AFRICAN HONEY-HARISSA ROASTED SALMON

This recipe doesn't need an abundance of ingredients since they provide a contrast of spicy and sweet flavors. The harissa will steep everything in a fiery orange hue.

Makes: 3-4 Servings

Cooking + Prep Time: 40 minutes

Ingredients:

•4 & 1/2 lb. of skin-on salmon fillets

•2 tbsp. of oil, olive

•Salt, kosher

•1/2 cup of honey, pure

•2 tsp. of harissa

Instructions:

1. Preheat broiler.

2. Rub salmon using oil. Season as desired. Place on rimmed cookie sheet with foil lining. Broil in top 1/3 of oven for 8-10 minutes.

3. Whisk harissa and honey together in medium bowl, creating the glaze.

4. Salmon will start turning gold after broiling for 10 minutes. Brush majority of glaze on salmon. Reserve a little bit for glossing later on.

5. Broil salmon for 5 more minutes after glazing. Baste glaze over salmon 1-2 times while it is cooking. Remove salmon from oven. Pour remainder of glaze over fillets. Serve.

22

TUNISIAN VEGETABLE-FISH STEW

This cumin and garlic tomato broth gives veggies and fish a suitable place for simmering. The pepper flakes provide a wonderful spiciness.

Makes: 4 Servings

Cooking + Prep Time: 50 Minutes

Ingredients:

- •2 tbsp. of oil, cooking
- •1 chopped onion, medium
- •4 thinly sliced garlic cloves
- •3 tbsp. of tomato paste, no salt added

•1 & 1/2 tsp. of cumin, ground
•1/4 tsp. of pepper flakes, red, dried
•1/2 tsp. of pepper, ground
•1 tsp. of salt, kosher
•1 quart of chicken broth, canned, low sodium
•2 peeled, 1" cubed potatoes, boiling type
•3 carrots, medium, cut in 1" cubes
•1 peeled, 1" cubed turnip, medium
•2 x 1"-cubed zucchini
•1 & 1/2 lb. of 1" cubed cod fillets
•3 tbsp. of chopped parsley, fresh

Instructions:

1. In large-sized pot, heat oil on med-low. Add garlic and onion. Stir occasionally while cooking for 3-5 minutes, till onion becomes translucent.

2. Add and stir tomato paste, pepper flakes, cumin, 1/2 tsp. kosher salt & pepper. Stir while cooking for 2-3 minutes.

3. Add broth. Bring to simmer. Add carrots and potatoes. Simmer for 8-10 minutes. Add and stir in zucchini, turnip & last 1/2 tsp. of kosher salt. Simmer 10 more minutes.

4. Add cod and bring back up to simmer. Cook 2-3 minutes, till barely done. Top stew with parsley and serve.

23

NORTH AFRICAN HONEY & SAFFRON ROAST CHICKEN

This chicken dish is inspired by the cooks of Morocco. It's simple to make yet still beautiful enough for holiday gatherings or dinner parties.

Makes: 4-6 Servings

Cooking + Prep Time: 1 hour & 35 minutes + 1 hour or overnight marinating time

Ingredients:
- 1 quartered chicken, large
- 2 coarsely chopped onions, medium
- 4 tbsp. of oil, olive

- 1 tsp. of ginger, ground
- 1 tsp. of cinnamon, ground
- 1 generous pinch saffron threads
- 1 lemon, fresh, juice only
- 4 tbsp. of water, cold
- 2 tsp. of sea salt, coarse
- 1 tsp. of pepper, ground
- 3/4 cup of hazel nuts, unskinned
- 3 & 1/2 tbsp. of honey, pure
- 2 tbsp. of water, rose
- 2 coarsely chopped onions, green

Instructions:

1. In large-sized bowl, mix pieces of chicken with oil, onions, cinnamon, ginger, lemon juice, saffron, water, sea salt & ground pepper. Allow to marinate in refrigerator for an hour minimum, or overnight.

2. Preheat oven to 375F. Spread hazel nuts on cookie sheet. Toast in oven till browned lightly, 10 minutes. Coarsely chop nuts and set them aside.

3. Transfer chicken with marinade to rimmed cookie sheet or baking pan. Arrange pieces of chicken with the skin side facing up. Cook in 375F oven for 30-35 minutes.

4. Mix rose water, honey & nuts, making a paste. Remove chicken from oven. Spoon nut paste over all pieces. Return to oven for 5-10 minutes till chicken has cooked fully through with no pink remaining. Nuts should be golden brown.

5. Transfer chicken to serving platter. Use green onion pieces to garnish. Serve.

24

MOROCCAN VEGETABLE CURRY

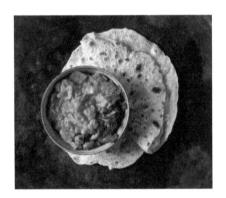

This curry is filled with tasty vegetables! It makes a wonderful meal served over rice, and you can use ginger-carrot juice instead of orange juice if you prefer.

Makes: 6 Servings

Cooking + Prep Time: 55 minutes

Ingredients:

- •1 peeled, cubed sweet potato, medium
- •1 cubed eggplant, medium
- •1 chopped bell pepper, green
- •1 chopped bell pepper, red

- 2 chopped carrots, medium
- 1 chopped onion, sweet
- 6 tbsp. of oil, olive
- 3 minced garlic cloves
- 1 tsp. of turmeric, ground
- 1 tbsp. of curry powder, spicy
- 1 tsp. of cinnamon, ground
- 3/4 tbsp. of salt, sea
- 3/4 tsp. of pepper, cayenne
- 1 x 15-oz. can of drained garbanzo beans
- 1/2 cup of almonds, blanched
- 1 sliced zucchini, medium
- 2 tbsp. of raisins, dark or golden
- 1 cup of orange juice, fresh squeezed
- 10 oz. of spinach, fresh

Instructions:

1. In large pot, place the eggplant, sweet potato, carrots, peppers, onions & 3 tbsp. of oil. Sauté on med. heat for 3-5 minutes.

2. In medium pan, place 3 tbsp. oil, turmeric, garlic, cinnamon, curry powder, sea salt & cayenne pepper. Sauté on med. for 3-4 minutes.

3. Pour spiced garlic mixture in pot with the vegetables. Add garbanzo beans, zucchini, almonds, orange juice and raisins. Cover and simmer for 15-20 minutes.

4. Add the spinach to the pot. Cook for 5 minutes more. Serve.

25

NORTH AFRICAN GINGER, CARROT & HARISSA SOUP

Harissa is a spicy paste that is often a part of North African dishes. The level of heat does vary from brand to brand, so check at international stores or online to find one suitable for your family's tastes.

Makes: 4-6 Servings

Cooking + Prep Time: 35 minutes

Ingredients:

- •8 tbsp. of oil, olive
- •Pale green & white parts of 1 leek, sliced finely
- •1 chopped onion, small
- •2 tsp. of thinly sliced garlic

- •1 x 2" knob of peeled, finely chopped ginger, fresh
- •1 tsp. of cumin seed, ground
- •1/2 tsp. of coriander, ground
- •1-2 tbsp. of harissa paste, your choice of heat level
- •2 & 1/2 lb. of peeled, roughly chopped carrots
- •1 & 1/2 quarts of broth, chicken or vegetable, low sodium
- •Salt, kosher, as desired
- •1/4 cup of pine nuts, toasted
- •2 tbsp. of chopped parsley leaves, fresh
- •2 tbsp. lemon juice & 1 tbsp. of zest from 1 fresh lemon

Instructions:

1. Heat 2 tbsp. oil in large pan on med. heat till it shimmers. Add the onions, leeks, ginger and garlic. Stir frequently while cooking for 3-5 minutes, till vegetables have softened but have not yet browned.

2. Add harissa paste, cumin and coriander. Stir constantly while cooking for a minute or so, till fragrant. Add carrots. Stir, coating in spiced mixture.

3. Add the broth and 1 pinch kosher salt. Bring to boil. Reduce to low simmer. Stir occasionally while cooking for 18-20 minutes, till carrots are fully tender.

4. Heat 2 tbsp. oil in small-sized skillet on med. heat till it shimmers. Add the pine nuts and reduce heat level to low. Toss and stir constantly while cooking for 8-10 minutes, till nutty brown and fragrant. Transfer to large bowl. Allow to cool for a minute or two. Stir in pinch of kosher salt, then parsley and lemon zest.

5. As soon as the carrots become tender, transfer 1/2 of soup to food processor. Blend on low speed first, and work your way to high speed. With food processor still running on high, drizzle in 2 tbsp. of oil slowly.

6. Transfer soup to clean, large pot. Press it through fine strainer, as desired. Repeat the blending with the rest of the soup, adding last 2 tbsp. oil. When soup is all pureed, add kosher salt as desired. Whisk in the fresh lemon juice. Top with parsley and pine nut mixture and serve promptly.

DELECTABLE DESSERT RECIPES FROM NORTH AFRICA

26

TUNISIAN ALMOND DESSERT BALLS

This almond treat is known in Tunisia as Kaber Ellouz. You'll braid three pieces of the almond dough together, each one in a different color, to make the dessert.

Makes: 12 Servings

Cooking + Prep Time: 35 minutes

Ingredients:

- 3/4 cup of sugar, caster
- 2 tsp. of sugar, vanilla
- 7 tbsp. of water, filtered
- 4 tsp. of rose water
- 2 & 1/2 cups of meal, almond

•1/2 tsp. of food color, red
•1/2 tsp. of food color, green
For garnishing
•Sugar, superfine & pine nuts, as desired

Instructions:

1. In small pan, combine the sugar with vanilla sugar. Stir in water. Head on med. Whisk occasionally while cooking for 10-12 minutes, till sugar has dissolved. Add rose water and whisk it in well.

2. Pour almond meal into med. bowl. Stir in the syrup with wooden spoon. After dough is coming together, knead it on a dusted work surface till you have a smooth texture.

3. Divide dough in three pieces of equal size. Knead red coloring into first, green coloring into second and leave last piece without color.

4. Roll pieces into 3/4" wide ropes. Place side by side. Braid them together. Push braid together, sealing it. Cut in 1" pieces. Roll pieces into balls.

5. Sprinkle some of the superfine sugar on large plate. Roll balls in sugar and then place them on platter. Use pine nuts for sprinkling, as desired. Serve.

27

MOROCCAN ROSE, RHUBARB & GINGER CRUMBLE

This amazing recipe offers you many textures and flavors. It's at once creamy, crumbly, sweet, sour and fragrant. You can serve it with labneh yogurt if you like.

Makes: 6 Servings

Cooking + Prep Time: 1 hour & 50 minutes

Ingredients:

•1 lb. of rhubarb, fresh

•To grease pan: 2 & 1/2 tsp. of butter, unsalted

•9 tsp. of finely chopped stem, ginger

For the jar: 3 tbsp. of syrup

•5 tbsp. of sugar, light brown

•2 tsp. of rose water

•1 pinch of salt, kosher

•7 oz. of flour, plain

•1/2 tsp. of ginger, ground

•4 & 1/2 oz. of unsalted butter, cold

•2 & 1/2 oz. of sugar, caster

For serving as desired: ice cream, custard, Greek yogurt or labneh yogurt

Instructions:

1. Preheat the oven to 400F. Grease oven-proof 8-inch casserole dish with butter. Set it aside.

2. Trim rhubarb ends. Slice into 1" pieces. Transfer rhubarb to large bowl. Add syrup, ginger stem, rose water and brown sugar. Combine ingredients well. Set bowl aside.

3. To a separate bowl, add flour, salt and ginger. Remove cold butter from refrigerator. Cut in 1/3-inch pieces. Use fingertips to rub flour into butter till mixture has the appearance of breadcrumbs. Add sugar. Mix, combining well.

4. Transfer rhubarb mixture to greased casserole dish. Sprinkle crumbly mixture on top. Cover all of the rhubarb with crumbles.

5. Bake in 400F oven for 40-45 minutes, till crumbles are golden and rhubarb has softened. Serve while warm with toppings of your choice from above.

28

SNACK SIZED CASHEW BAKLAVA

This recipe is a tweak on traditional baklava, which is made in large layered trays full of goodness. In the recipe, the dough is molded into smooth long cigar-shaped pieces and filled with brown sugar and cashews.

Makes: 4-6 Servings

Cooking + Prep Time: 2 hours & 20 minutes

Ingredients:

•1 stick + 6 tbsp. of melted butter, unsalted

•6 oz. of cashews

- •6 tbsp. of packed brown sugar, light
- •1/2 tsp. of cinnamon, ground
- •1/2 tsp. of salt, kosher
- •1/2 cup of sugar, granulated
- •1/2 lemon zest, grated finely
- •2 tbsp. of lemon juice, fresh
- •3 each of 13"x16" phyllo sheets

Instructions:

1. Preheat oven to 350F.

2. In food processor, combine 6 tbsp. of butter with cashews, cinnamon, brown sugar & salt. Pulse till filling has been chopped finely.

3. In small pan, combine 1/4 cup of filtered water with sugar. Bring to boil. Stir while cooking for 2-3 minutes, till sugar has dissolved. Remove syrup from heat. Stir in lemon juice and zest. Allow mixture to set for 12-15 minutes.

4. Pour lemony syrup through fine sieve into glass measuring cup. Allow it to cool. Discard remainder.

5. Grease 8" square baking pan (metal) with some of melted butter still left. On work surface, lay a sheet of phyllo so short sides lay parallel to you. Brush with butter and place second sheet on top of first.

6. Brush phyllo with melted butter. Cover with third sheet of phyllo. Brush last sheet of phyllo with butter. Cut stack of phyllo sheets lengthways in halves. Cut those rectangles crossways in 5 small, equal-sized rectangles.

7. Arrange 2 tbsp. of cashew filling in line along longer edge of one phyllo rectangle. Roll phyllo dough around filling into log shape. Place in baking pan prepared above. Repeat with the rest of the phyllo and filling, making nine additional logs. Arrange them against others, fitting snugly in one layer in prepared pan.

8. Brush remainder of butter on top of logs. Bake in 350F oven for 30-35 minutes, till crisp and light brown in color.

9. Remove pan from oven. Pour cooled syrup atop and over logs of baklava. Allow to cool. Invert logs and allow them to stand for 12-15 minutes, so syrup penetrates all areas. Serve.

29

MATCHA GHRIBA WITH WALNUTS

These ghribas are similar to power balls, and the matcha makes them even better. This is a quick and simple recipe, and it will be especially tasty if you're a fan of matcha tea.

Makes: 12 Servings

Cooking + Prep Time: 55 minutes

Ingredients:

- •5 & 1/3 oz. of powdered walnuts
- •3 & 1/2 oz. of powdered almonds

•2 & 3/4 oz. of sugar, caster

•1/2 tbsp. of softened butter, unsalted

•1/2 tbsp. of jam, apricot

•1 tbsp. of tea powder, matcha green

•1 egg, large

•1 tsp. of baking powder, heaping

•To coat cookies: 5 & 1/3 oz. of sugar, icing

Instructions:

1. Preheat the oven to 350F.

2. In large-sized bowl, use spatula or your hands and mix all ingredients except icing sugar, till you have a slightly sticky, smooth dough.

3. Divide dough by hand in 12 balls, about 1" in diameter.

4. Roll balls in the icing sugar till coated completely.

5. Transfer cookies to lined cookie sheet. Press cookies lightly but don't flatten them.

6. Place cookie sheet in oven. Bake at 350F for 10-13 minutes, till cookies become firm & cracked on outsides.

7. Allow cookies to cool for 15 minutes, then transfer to wire rack so they can finish cooling. Serve.

30

LEBANESE SHORTBREAD COOKIES

Known in Lebanon as Ma'amoul bil Tamer, these festive cookies are scented with orange and rose blossom waters. The nutmeg and cinnamon-spiced filling makes them irresistible.

Makes: 24 Servings +/-

Cooking + Prep Time: 50 minutes + 2 & 1/2 hours chilling time

Ingredients:

For crust:

• 3 cups of semolina, fine
• 1/2 cup of flour, all-purpose
• 12 tbsp. of melted, cooled butter, unsalted

• 3 tbsp. of sugar, granulated
• 1/2 tsp. of salt, kosher
• 1/3 cup of milk, whole
• 2 & 1/2 tbsp. of water, rose
• 2 tsp. of water, orange blossom

For filling:

• 5 cups of dates, pitted
• 10 tbsp. of cubed, chilled butter, unsalted
• 2 tbsp. of cinnamon, ground
• 1 & 1/2 tbsp. of nutmeg, grated

Instructions:

1. To prepare crust, pulse the flour, semolina, sugar, butter & kosher salt in food processor, till they form pea-sized crumbles. Then add orange and rose blossom waters and milk. Pulse till you have formed a dough. Flatten the dough in a disc. Wrap in cling wrap and place in refrigerator for 2 hours to chill.

2. To prepare filling, puree the butter, dates, nutmeg and cinnamon in cleaned food processor till smooth. Divide in 25 balls and allow to chill in refrigerator for 1/2 hour.

3. Heat the oven to 400F. Divide the dough in 25 balls. Press finger into one dough ball and make a pocket. Place a ball of the filling into that pocket. Pinch the sides, encasing the filling, then roll into ball. Use your palm to flatten the ball a bit. Repeat with remainder of dough and filling.

4. Transfer balls to cookie sheet. Bake in 400F oven for 20 to 25 minutes, till golden. Allow them to cool and then serve.

CONCLUSION

This North Africa cookbook has shown you…

How to use different ingredients to affect unique exotic tastes in many types of the dishes.

How can you include North African recipes in your home repertoire?

You can…

• Make an egg and bean breakfast or tahini fava bean breakfast, which you may not have heard of them before. They are just as mouthwatering tasty as they sound.

• Cook the soups and stews, which are widely served in North African homes. Find their ingredients in meat & produce or frozen food sections of your local grocery stores.

• Enjoy making African seafood dishes, including shrimp & tilapia. Fish is a mainstay in the recipes year-round, and there are SO many ways to make it great.

• Make the dishes using potatoes and other vegetables in North African recipes. There is something about them that makes them such comforting dishes.

• Make the desserts as ginger crumble and matcha ghriba, which are tasty and tempting for your dinner guests.

Conclusion

Share the special recipes with your friends!

Ingram Content Group UK Ltd.
Milton Keynes UK
UKHW020608200723
425487UK00008B/37